BROKEN PIECES

VINAMRA TIWARI

ISBN 979-888569849-8

For my parents and sister

Contents

Acknowledgements   *vii*

Preface   *ix*

1. Broken   1

Cold

The Eyes That Lost Their Light

Hatred From My Love

Conflict

Spark Of Love

Remember?

Memories

Moving On

2. Lonely   19

Stars

A Silent Wish

The Cold Clock

The Gleam Of Hope

Escape

I Wonder...

When Will The Rain Stop?

Hidden Tears

Diary

3. Finding Love   39

Hope

Starry Night

Contents

Still Searching

Bottled Up Emotions

The World Is Still Alive

Pain

A Stranger's Warmth

Those Blissful Words

Together

Broken Pieces

Whole

A Message From The Poet

Conclusion   65

Acknowledgements

I would like to express my gratitude towards my parents who have helped and supported me in every possible way so that I could be successful in making this book a reality.

Secondly, I am extremely grateful to my sister who has designed the cover page of this book and gave my book a face.

I would like to thank my editor Sakina Rizvi as well who has been a great help to me in bringing those small errors to my attention.

Preface

A collection of poems which depicts several feelings and emotions which an average person goes through in his/her everyday life.

The poems in this book are written in a manner in which the reader finds no difficulty in relating to and immersing themselves in it.

1. broken

cold

and tonight amidst the cold

I stood watching you

the warmth of your embrace

I longed for

if only you weren't so far

the eyes that lost their light

you shone bright

like moon in the night

I looked up to you

with eyes filled with love and colour

When did you learn to steal?

rob me of my eyes

I looked up to you

with eyes not the same

I looked up to you

with eyes tainted with hate

I looked up to you

with eyes who have lost their light.

hatred from my love

I hated every moment

I was in love with you

your soft voice like velvet

felt harsh and unbearable

I hated myself

for I was in love with you

for I knew

you were using me

that I was just a time-pass

but O'me O'life

I was in love

and I hated you.

conflict

Living with you

was like living

with a heart that

wants to live

but a mind

that wants to die

how did I come

to be like this-

my heart wants to stay

while my mind wants to run away

spark of love

You sparked something in my heart

which burned down

my walls and my life

You sparked something in my heart

which burned down

both you and me

And there in the ashes of our love

you lay with your stone cold body

facing towards the sky

How bright we used to burn.

Now, look at you

and look at me.

remember?

do you remember

how wide I used

to smile

do you remember

my eyes which used

to shine like stars

do you remember

all the dreams

I used to have

do you remember

all the pain

that you gave

do you remember

the sound of my cries

on those sleepless nights

do you remember

my dear, all the

things you stole

memories

memories of a time

long forgotten

come to haunt me

at night

sometimes I wonder

If I made

the right choice

by giving you

the key to my heart

and mind.

moving on

I looked at you

and you looked at me

and I remember the day

we first kissed

images flashed through my mind

memories of that day

but today I let them flow

today I didn't run away

I looked at you

and you looked at me

but today I went past you

without looking back.

2. lonely

stars

like white little dots

sewn on a curtain of dark

were the friends of a boy

who looked up in the sky

He would whisper secrets to them

for they were his treasure keepers

in a world full of strangers.

a silent wish

the patter of rain

the screams of clouds

growling and shaking the sky

threatening to tear the heavens apart.

somewhere amidst the thunder and rain

a boy peering through his classroom window

wished for the rain to never stop

as it dampened the voice of those around him.

the cold clock

The cold bleak atmosphere

is nothing compared to my skin

I am familiar with the

dark corners of my bed

wherein I lay alone

looking at the ceiling

Lonely- however I may

the clock keeps me company

Tick-tock the sound of the clock

each passing second

each passing moment

I closed my eyes

and drifted- to a world no one knows of

to a world where she was waiting

Tick-tock the sound of the clock

was now fading and fading

until all that left was silence

I took my final breath

and drifted- to the world no one knows of.

the gleam of hope

Hope

in this bleak world

has a slim chance

you find it

only to cherish it in your hands

for but a few

precious moments

you find it

when your feet have almost gotten torn

from all the running

and chasing after its gleam

you find it

only for its shine to reach you

and your hand to

just reach it

you find it

only to see it

lost and taken

again.

escape

It is

when I lay my head

on the pillow

that I escape the sleepless nights

It is

when the arms of sleep

take me far from here

that I find calm

In a world unknown

It is

when I dive deep

into the ocean of my sleep

that I can escape my thoughts.

I wonder...

sometimes I wonder

if I'll ever find a love

that'll rekindle

the cold heart of mine

just enough so that

we can both share

from its warmth.

when will the rain stop?

drops of rain fell

on my warm skin

it was cold that night

I strolled down the lifeless alley

with my now cold body

I was drenched, almost completely

The rain fell from the clouds

which hid the stars and the moon

drops of rain fell

on the broken path

on which I walked

How ironical I wondered

that the beautiful nature

which heals the wounds of the many

is acting as a metaphor for the

bleakness and pain in my life

Drops of rain fell

and I kept on walking

but the rain never stopped

just like my pain

just like my pain.

hidden tears

countless souls in doom

putting up their happy faces

still.

I wonder if they are

betraying the world or themselves

by showing their smiles

with tears hidden beneath their eyes.

diary

pages by pages

I flipped

through my diary

with a pen in hand

and the paper beneath

thinking of the

stars and the seas,

of wonderful oceans

and the calm breeze

but all I could

ever make out

from what I wrote

was a man in pain

who felt just like me.

3. finding love

hope

words were all I heard

in a voice of velvet

a sea of words

dragging me in

drowning my conscious self

I succumbed to the

image of the world

until I looked up and saw the shining stars

and a golden orb

and some light far-off

from a distant land

hit like a spear to my heart

and rekindled a small spot

in the darkest corners of my heart

and I named it hope.

starry night

the night sky full of stars

over 'em the golden orb

outshining 'em all

when one day

a wind went past

cloudy skies overhead

stole that which

once lay still

now was gone.

still searching

like a breeze you went by

swiftly and sneakily

stole what was

beneath my chest

like a maniac I searched

but that breeze

never returned.

bottled up emotions

bottled up emotions broke free

when the light of her sight

reached his pallid eyes

emotions like a bottle of ink

broke

and spilled upon the paper

and a far off world was

carved

from the pieces of

the broken glass

and the paper

like his eyes

wasn't pallid anymore.

the world is still alive

How ironical right?

that all the world's emotions

are kept alive-

not in big labyrinthine cities

but in small little conversations

of two random strangers at night

who met by chance

on one gloomy day

where she couldn't be herself

and I couldn't be mine

When all the eyes

fell asleep

she radiated a light

which lit up faraway cities

and I carved stories for her

which was our little secret

for the night belonged to us

and we had found ourselves

strangers no more

she was herself

and I was mine.

pain

broken was her heart by many

trampled upon the pieces

by the same people

with whom she once shared

the love with

"share your pain with me"

I said to her

and I'll share your words

and the words will

transcend the world

broken feelings

and broken parts

the pain lingers

there in your heart

Spit it out

and I'll write it down

Spit it out

and I'll take it from you.

a stranger's warmth

how ironical it is

that the most beautiful words

are spoken

by the most broken hearts

shards of love

broken into infinite pieces

those delicate threads

who would've thought

would leave imperishable scars

healed only

by a stranger's warmth.

those blissful words

conversations with you

never seem to end

one after the other

a new one breaks out

and we'd chat

till the night goes out

and in doing so

every night I changed

little by little

you changed me

and filled me with the sound

of your sweet voice

like a blanket over my head

you gave me warmth

and rekindled the fire

which was long gone.

together

countless cold nights

I have spent alone

with no one

to share the pain

then I saw you

silent as a statue

with no one

to talk to

the words-

I shared with you

have now become

beautiful memories

You took my pain

and I took your silence

and together we fixed each other

from the broken pieces

of our forgotten past.

broken pieces

pieces by pieces

I made you and

you made me

broken were

both of us

it was you

who fixed me

and I

who fixed you

Whole

the warmth of

your embrace

now I can feel

It's my heart's

rekindled fire

which douses

tonight's cold

I looked up in the sky

and waved at my friends

but tonight I was not alone

tonight I felt whole.

a message from the poet

sometimes your life

gets tough

sometimes your plans

don't work

sometimes your dreams

fall apart

But-

never has it happened

that you aren't

given a choice

a choice

to build things up

a choice

to plan things out

a choice

to dream again

a choice-

to let the 'choice'

slip out of your hand

or grasp it tight.

Conclusion

This book took me quite some time to write and the experience and joy I got from writing this book is unparalleled.

Poetry has always been my passion since I was 15 years old. The process of converting emotions and feelings into words is something I am drawn towards a lot. And this book provided me with an opportunity to do the same and connect with the people world-wide as well.

I would like to thank all of my friends who have helped and supported me because without their support, this book would not have been possible.